SITTING BULL

Warrior of the Sioux

by Jane Fleischer
illustrated by Bert Dodson

Troll Associates

Troll Associates,
Library of Congress Catalog Card Number: 78-18047
ISBN 0-89375-144-8

10 9 8 7 6 5 4 3

SITTING BULL

Warrior of the Sioux

SASKATCHEWAN

MANITOBA

SIOUX MIGRATE
NORTH

BUFORD

MONTANA

NORTH DAKOTA

LITTLE BIG HORN

STANDING
ROCK
RESERVATION

SOUTH DAKOTA

BIG HORN
MOUNTAINS

BLACK HILLS

WYOMING

North Platte River

NEBRASKA

LARAMIE

TREATY
1868

Platte River

South Platte River

COLORADO

It was a moonless night, dark enough for the Sioux warriors to surprise their enemies, the Crows.

Slow stood silently as his father rode away without him. They had named him Slow when he was small because he had spoken slowly, eaten slowly, and grown slowly. But now he had seen fourteen winters. Now he was ready to earn a warrior's name.

It was time. He would not be slow to show his courage!

Slow painted his body with red war paint. Then he mounted his small gray pony and followed the dusty trail of the warriors.

The braves in the war party laughed to see a boy dressed for war.

But his father did not laugh. Proudly, he gave his brave son his own "coup" stick. Then the laughter stopped.

Every warrior knew that to touch an enemy with this stick took as much courage as to kill!

Silently, they waited as the Crows came closer and closer.

Slow could hardly wait. At the signal, he raced like lightning, ahead of the others.

When the Crows saw the strength of their enemies, they quickly turned to escape. Slow drove his pony as hard as he could. His heart pounded as he leaned forward and struck a Crow warrior.

"On-hey!" he shouted. "I, Slow, have conquered him!"

Soon, the battle was done. The Crows had been defeated.

At dawn, the Sioux braves returned to their village. They had horses, weapons, and a new warrior.

Slow sat tall and proud on his new bay horse. He wore a gold eagle feather in his hair. The bright feather showed that he had counted his first coup.

That night, the drums beat a song of victory. Then his father gave him a warrior's name, and the boy danced wildly with happiness.

From that night on, he was called Sitting Bull. In years to come, he would make that name famous.

Sitting Bull's people, the Sioux, were always on the move. They followed the great herds of buffalo across the wide plains of the Dakota country.

Buffalo meat fed them. Buffalo hides covered their tepees. Buffalo skins made robes, shields, and drums. Buffalo bones and horns made cups, dishes, tools, and toys. Buffalo ribs made sleds. Buffalo chips fueled their fires. No part of the buffalo was wasted. For the Sioux, the buffalo was the "giver of life."

10

Hunting buffalo was dangerous but exciting. Sitting Bull was always ready to ride after the shaggy, hump-backed beasts.

He was always ready for battle, too!

The Sioux did not welcome strangers to their hunting grounds. They fought anyone who dared to cross Sioux lands.

As Sitting Bull grew to manhood, he counted coup many times. He captured many fine horses and guns. It was not long before he wore the feathers and buffalo-horn hat of the warrior society, the Strong Hearts.

One night, in a fierce battle against the Crows, Sitting Bull was wounded badly. But pain did not stop him. He rushed forward and killed the Crows' Chief!

From that time on, Sitting Bull walked with a limp. But his bravery was rewarded. At their victory dance, the warriors made him Chief of the Strong Hearts!

In time, Sitting Bull became Chief of his tribe, the Hunkpapa. This was one of the many Sioux tribes that lived on the Great Plains.

The Hunkpapas held the best hunting grounds. For a long time, they saw little of the white man's wagons.

Other tribes of the Great Sioux Nation were not so lucky. To the east and the south, scattered tribes of Sioux had seen wagons belonging to miners, settlers, and soldiers ruin their hunting grounds. Their arrows could not hold back the endless stream of covered wagons.

Some Indians began to take up the white man's ways. But many decided to leave their lands.

Sitting Bull could not turn his back on his Indian brothers. His people shared food, clothing, and tepees with the tribes that came north.

The seasons passed. Then more trouble came.

The wagons began to travel through Hunkpapa territory. Many people came to settle on Sioux land. Soldiers came with guns that roared like thundering herds of buffalo. The soldiers built forts to protect the new settlers.

14

Time after time, Sioux war parties attacked the wagon trains. Still, the wagons kept coming.

In the summer of 1867, the scattered tribes of the Sioux Nation gathered together. They knew they must stand together to save their land.

Many Chiefs sat together at the council fire. For the first time in their long history, they must choose one mighty Chief to lead them all.

Sitting Bull's fame had spread to the tepees of many tribes. He was a fearless fighter; yet he had shown kindness to the poor and homeless. All the Chiefs agreed that Sitting Bull was the one to lead them.

Sitting Bull was proud to wear the beautiful Chief's headdress of black and white eagle feathers. Each feather stood for a brave deed done by the best warriors of the Sioux Nation. Now, the headdress was a sign of their joining together to serve the whole Sioux Nation.

Sitting Bull knew it would be his duty to see that his people were not hungry. He knew if he spoke for war, they would fight. If he spoke for peace, they would follow.

He wanted nothing to do with the white men. He did not want war or friendship. He only wanted his people to be left alone.

The government in Washington was troubled by the fighting with the Great Plains Indians, so a new treaty was made in 1868 in Laramie. This agreement gave the Sioux a large territory of their own in the Black Hills. Every hill from north of the Platte River and east of the Big Horn Mountains was Indian land.

With the signing of the treaty, Sitting Bull's hopes soared like an eagle!

Now, he thought, perhaps the wagons will never again trample the grass of the Sioux hunting grounds.

At last the Northern Plains were peaceful. In their sacred Black Hills, the Sioux sang songs of joy to the Great Spirit.

Sitting Bull looked out across the plains as the tribes scattered to their old hunting grounds. He knew that peace was the greatest victory a Chief could win for his people. He prayed that the peace would last.

But in less than six winters, the promises made at Laramie had been broken.

"Gold! There's gold in the Black Hills!"

Nothing would hold back the miners with their dreams of riches. The treaty meant little to them.

Now, Bluecoats rode into the sacred lands. Word came that the American government wanted to buy the Black Hills.

"Never!" said Sitting Bull. "This land belongs to the Sioux. If the outsiders try to take it, we will fight!"

Puffs of smoke sent signals across the plains. Soon, every trail led to the camp of Sitting Bull.

Never before had so many Indians gathered together. Thousands of Sioux, Cheyenne, Arapaho, and Blackfoot warriors sang songs of war.

For many days, the warriors danced the sacred Sun Dance. As the tom-toms beat, Sitting Bull danced and prayed. Finally, he could dance no more. His men carried him to his tepee.

That night he had a strange dream. In it he saw Bluecoats falling from the sky into the Indians' camp. In his dream he saw a great victory for his people.

Soon afterward, when General George Crook led more than a thousand men into the Rosebud Valley, Indian scouts saw the dust rise from the long line of soldiers. The signals for war came to Sitting Bull's camp.

The warriors were ready. They rode out to battle.

General Crook never reached Sitting Bull's camp. By sundown, many Bluecoats had fallen, and General Crook rode away in defeat.

Sitting Bull warned his men that more Bluecoats would come.

"This was not the battle in my dream," he said. "The Bluecoats will come into our camp. We must stay together. We must be ready."

Seven days passed. Sitting Bull moved his camp to the valley of the Little Big Horn River. A city of tepees stood side by side in wide circles.

At noon on the eighth day, the peace was broken with a cry of alarm. Warriors on the hillside shouted, "Bluecoats! Many Bluecoats!"

Colonel George A. Custer led the fateful charge. He had been warned that his men were badly outnumbered. But Custer had dreams of great glory. He was determined to defeat the mighty Chief Sitting Bull. He wanted this battle to make him famous.

Bullets and arrows flew. War cries filled the air.

The battle was fierce and terrible, but it did not last long.

In a very short time, Colonel Custer and all his men were dead.

By late summer, the Indians had killed more than a thousand soldiers. Sitting Bull knew that these were great victories, but he also knew that more Bluecoats would come. Bluecoats on ponies, Bluecoats on foot, Bluecoats with cannons would come endlessly onto Indian lands.

With each moon, the buffalo were harder to find. Sitting Bull's people must be fed.

Though it made his heart heavy to think of leaving his land, Sitting Bull knew that he and his people must go.

At the council fire, the Chiefs could not agree. Some wanted to stay and fight. Others said they would go south. Before long, the tribes had scattered in many directions.

Sitting Bull decided to lead the Hunkpapas north to Canada. With the winter coming upon them, they sadly left their sacred Black Hills.

In Canada, where the English ruled, Sitting Bull found peace for his people. But planting crops and living in one place was not the way of the Sioux. Now they had no hunting ground of their own.

To the south, the Bluecoats had burned the grass the buffalo ate. They killed the great animals by the thousands.

Sitting Bull's people were hungry and poor. Food became more scarce. They longed for their old life on the plains.

Sitting Bull feared his people would die of hunger.

In 1878, messengers came to Canada from the government in Washington. They brought new promises of peace, food, and a reservation.

Sitting Bull did not believe them. He was sure that if he crossed the line, they would kill him.

But as the seasons passed, he faced the sad truth. His people were starving. As Chief, he must lead them back into the land of their birth.

On a hot July day in 1881, Sitting Bull rode into Fort Buford in North Dakota to surrender.

He was no longer young and strong. His tired face showed the hardships of the long, difficult years.

Sitting Bull felt a great sadness. He stood on Dakota ground, but he was no longer free. His young men would not live as hunters and do brave deeds. The government would close them up in a reservation. Now, his people would have to travel the white man's path.

"Let it be known," he sadly said, "that I, Sitting Bull, was the last man of my people to lay down my gun."

For two years, the great leader of the Sioux
Nation was kept a prisoner of the government.
What remained of the Hunkpapa tribe was sent
to the Standing Rock Reservation.

Finally, Sitting Bull was allowed to return to his people. He found them hungry and cold. Long seasons without rain had turned the soil to dust. There were no buffalos for meat. There was no-where to go.

The government had promised the Indians cattle, tools, and wagons. Again, Sitting Bull reminded the government agent, James McLaughlin, of these promises. But McLaughlin would do little to help.

To McLaughlin and the Bluecoats, Sitting Bull was nothing but a troublemaker.

In 1885, McLaughlin sent Sitting Bull to travel with Buffalo Bill's Wild West Show. The name of Sitting Bull was known throughout the land. Many people were curious to see what he looked like.

"Now," McLaughlin thought, "the Indians won't have their leader around to stir them up!"

In city after city, people packed the halls to see the old Chief.

Buffalo Bill wanted to take Sitting Bull to England, but the Chief had had enough of shows. He was not happy on the reservation, but he was not happy in the white man's world, either.

So he returned to his people.

McLaughlin was not pleased to have the old Chief back.

At Standing Rock, Sitting Bull found new trouble. Conditions had grown worse. Hunger and sickness were sweeping through Indian reservations all over the West.

Far away, in Nevada, a Paiute Indian called Wovoca dreamed of new hope for all Indians. He said that soon all the dead warriors would rise up. The buffalo would return, and the white men would leave the Indians' land forever.

43

The desperate people needed such a hope. Wovoca's word spread from one reservation to the next. Day after day, Indians danced and sang the sacred songs of the Ghost Dance. They thought it would bring back the old times of happiness and plenty.

Sitting Bull did not really believe such a dream, but many of his people did. He did not stop them from dancing.

Week after week, the loud drums and sad songs of the Ghost Dance echoed, like war songs, across the plains.

The settlers were frightened. The Bluecoats were worried, too.

By now, in Standing Rock, Indian had turned against Indian. Some Indians worked as soldiers to keep order among their own people.

The Bluecoats were ready for an uprising. They believed Sitting Bull would lead the Indians to war again.

On a cold winter night in December of 1890, McLaughlin sent a large party of Indian soldiers to bring Sitting Bull back, dead or alive!

Sitting Bull was pulled from his bed and out of his cabin.

Shouting in anger, his warriors rushed to save their Chief. The Indian soldiers pushed Sitting Bull toward his horse.

Suddenly, there was a single gunshot ... then another, and another!

When it was all over, fourteen men were dead. One of them was Sitting Bull.

47

With Sitting Bull's death, the Ghost Dances ended. Not long afterward, the Indian war drums were silenced at the Battle of Wounded Knee.

Towns and cities grew where tepees had stood. Trains rumbled across the trails where buffalo had grazed.

The old ways were gone. But the name of Sitting Bull was not forgotten.